Fragments of

Layers soft in muted tones,
Silent edges, echoes grown.
Fragments of a world once whole,
Each piece speaks, a calming soul.

Earth's embrace in gentle fold,
Stories of the brave and bold.
In every crack, a tale unfolds,
Faithful whispers, ages hold.

Stone's Silent Soliloquy

In silence deep, the stones confer,
Ancient voices softly stir.
Carved by time, they stand and wait,
Lessons learned, they softly state.

Beneath the sky, a patient grace,
Every line, a time-worn trace.
The solitude of earth's embrace,
In stony hearts, we find our place.

Original title:
Harmony in Stone

Copyright © 2024 Creative Arts Management OÜ
All rights reserved.

Author: Clement Portlander
ISBN HARDBACK: 978-9916-88-070-8
ISBN PAPERBACK: 978-9916-88-071-5

Interludes Carved in Quartz

Glistening dreams in quartz reside,
Whispers of time where secrets hide.
Trapped in light, a frozen dance,
Nature's art in a fleeting glance.

Crystalline tales of ages past,
Each mural formed, a shadow cast.
In radiant hues, they softly gleam,
Chasing echoes of a distant dream.

The Balance of Nature's Canvas

On the canvas of the earth below,
A blend of life in ebb and flow.
Colors shift with each new breath,
Harmony found in cycle of death.

Mountains rise and rivers bend,
Nature's tale in the world we tend.
In every stroke, a story spun,
The balance struck as hearts are one.

The Balance of Breath and Boulder

In the stillness, whispers flow,
Breath soft as a fading glow.
Boulders stand, steadfast and wide,
Nature's strength, our humble guide.

Each inhale, a gentle rise,
Inhale hope beneath the skies.
Exhale doubt, let it all roll,
Find the balance, mend the soul.

In the Shadows of Stalactites

Beneath the cave, where echoes dwell,
Whispers cling to every shell.
Stalactites hang, like ancient dreams,
Flowing softly in silver streams.

In shadowed corners, secrets keep,
Stories buried, deep and steep.
Glimmers dance on rocky walls,
Nature's symphony, it calls.

The Earth's Embrace

Roots stretch deep in sacred ground,
Every heartbeat is the sound.
The Earth, a mother, calm and vast,
Holding dreams from future and past.

In each crack, small flowers bloom,
Nature's magic dispels the gloom.
With every step, the soil sings,
Life awakens, on gentle wings.

Unbroken and Whole

In every shard of mortal glass,
Lies the beauty of the past.
Fragments shine in radiant light,
Unbroken spirits, ready to fight.

Together, we weave a bold thread,
From the words that often spread.
Hands united, hearts will warm,
In love's embrace, we find our form.

Reflections in the Stone

Glimmers hide in shadowed cracks,
Time unfolds in layered backs.
Thoughts entwined in silent grace,
Echoes dance in a timeless space.

Fossils trapped in memory's seam,
Whispers of a forgotten dream.
Nature's hand carves tales so bold,
In the heart of stone, life's stories told.

Each chisel's stroke, a lover's sigh,
Secrets held where echoes lie.
Hope and sorrow, a marriage true,
In the depths, all is renewed.

Underneath the sun's warm gleam,
Stones reflect the world's grand theme.
In every grain, a piece of soul,
Etched forever, the past's control.

Echoes of Earth's Embrace

Mighty mountains, guardians stand,
Cradled softly by nature's hand.
Whispering winds through ancient trees,
Serenade the world with ease.

Rivers flow with stories old,
Secrets in their depths, untold.
Pebbles sing of time long gone,
In the twilight, they carry on.

Beneath the moon's gentle glow,
Eternal rhythms ebb and flow.
Sculpted valleys, shadows weep,
Promises the earth shall keep.

When dawn breaks, colors ignite,
In every corner, pure delight.
Echoes linger, hearts embrace,
In this vast and sacred space.

Whispers of Ancient Quarried Dreams

In the depths of the rugged stone,
Lies a world all on its own.
Soft murmurs of the earth's deep past,
In every cleft, memories cast.

Dusty trails of artists' hands,
Chisel marks in quiet lands.
Shapes arise from quarry's gloom,
Awakening with life to bloom.

Fragments of a world once bright,
Whispers murmur in the night.
Silent guardians watch and keep,
Secrets that the stones still seep.

Holding on to what has been,
Dreams forever etched within.
Quarried dreams that softly call,
In their embrace, we find our all.

Serene Fantasies in Granite

Granite stillness, strong and true,
Crafted by the skies so blue.
In stillness lies a hidden peace,
Serenity, a sweet release.

Patterns carved in timeless stone,
Nature's magic, all alone.
Fantastical realms where spirits dwell,
In whispers, every secret tells.

Sunrise paints the stones with light,
Flecks of gold in morning's sight.
Merging shadows with the sun,
Serene fantasies have begun.

Echoes of the past arise,
In the granite, wisdom lies.
Chasing dreams through ages vast,
In every layer, the die is cast.

Cadence of the Canyon

Whispers rise from stone to sky,
Echoes of the past drift by.
Colors dance in dusk's embrace,
Nature's rhythm, a sacred place.

Winds weave tales through craggy halls,
Each pulse in rock, each shadow calls.
Footsteps linger on ancient trails,
Where time moves soft, and stillness sails.

The sun slips low, the shadows stretch,
In hues of gold, the world we sketch.
A symphony of earth and stone,
In each heartbeat, we find our own.

Resonance of the Riverbed

Beneath the surface, currents sway,
Soft whispers of the water play.
Pebbles shimmer in fleeting light,
As dreams meander, taking flight.

Gentle ripples kiss the shore,
Secrets shared, forevermore.
Reflections dance with the flowing stream,
Life unfolds as a tender dream.

In the stillness, time holds fast,
Each drop a tale, an echo cast.
Listen closely, hear the sound,
In the riverbed, peace is found.

Sculpted Tranquility

Carved by time, the rocks stand tall,
Silent witnesses to nature's call.
Mossy blankets cover stone,
In this stillness, we are never alone.

Gentle breezes whisper low,
Caressing all in softest flow.
Shapes emerge in varied hue,
Crafted gently, old yet new.

In every crevice, stories hide,
Of sun and rain, of time's great tide.
Beneath this dome of painted grace,
We find our hearts, our sacred space.

Balance Beneath the Surface

In still waters, calmness reigns,
Peaceful thoughts like gentle trains.
Beneath the waves, whispers dwell,
Secrets of the ocean's shell.

Currents weave a tale unseen,
A dance of life, serene, pristine.
Each movement hints at depths unknown,
In silence, truths are gently shown.

Roots entwined in muddy bed,
Finding balance where none's led.
In this dance of dark and light,
We learn to trust our inner sight.

Melodies of the Mountain

Whispers roam through ancient pines,
Echoes dance on clear blue skies.
Each note a story, softly shines,
In shadows where the silence lies.

Rivers hum a gentle tune,
Stars align in perfect grace.
Underneath the silver moon,
Nature's choir finds its place.

Footsteps tread on winding trails,
Harmony beneath each stone.
The wind carries forgotten tales,
In every heart, a song is sown.

Serenity Carved in Time

Moments slip like grains of sand,
Echoes of a quiet wish.
Life unfolds, a guiding hand,
In stillness, we find our bliss.

Whispers of the morning light,
Gentle glows on soft, wet ground.
In the calm, the heart takes flight,
With every breath, pure peace is found.

Time drips slowly, like a stream,
Each ripple tells a tale untold.
In this space, we dare to dream,
Serenity, both warm and bold.

Tones of the Timeless

In twilight's glow, the shadows play,
Colors blend in soft embrace.
Every hue, a song to say,
Life's vibrance found in every space.

Chorus of the stars above,
Celestial whispers weave the night.
Notes of warmth, a gentle love,
In stillness, we reach for the light.

Moments woven, thread by thread,
Capture echoes of the past.
In every glance, in words unsaid,
Timeless whispers, meant to last.

Unity of the Elements

Fire dances with an ardent grace,
Water flows in gentle streams.
Earth holds firm, a steadfast base,
Air carries the wisp of dreams.

Lightning strikes, a vibrant spark,
Thunder rolls in deep embrace.
Nature's rhythm knows no mark,
In harmony, we find our place.

Mountains rise, proud and tall,
Oceans pulse with ancient might.
We are one, in this grand hall,
Elements unite, wrongs made right.

Nature's Unspoken Language

In the whisper of the trees,
A secret song is sung.
Beneath the azure skies,
Old tales are still among.

The river flows in silence,
Carving rocks with grace.
Each ripple tells a story,
Of time and nature's pace.

Mountains stand as guardians,
Against the winds of change.
Their rugged peaks remember,
What we can't rearrange.

In every leaf and shadow,
Nature speaks so clear.
If we but pause and listen,
Her voice is always near.

Foundations of the Forgotten

In ruins, echoes linger,
Of lives once lived here bold.
Crumbled stones and whispers,
Tell stories long since told.

In the heart of the forest,
Old pathways weave and wind.
A past that breathes in silence,
With secrets intertwined.

Faded murals on the wall,
Show colors of the past.
Each brushstroke holds a memory,
Of moments meant to last.

Among the grave vines tangled,
Old voices gently call.
Their dreams, like distant shadows,
Are never lost at all.

Celestial Settlements

Stars like pinpricks glimmer,
In the velvet night's embrace.
Whispers of the cosmos,
Unfold in endless space.

Moons of silver dancing,
On tides of time and light.
Galaxies, vast and swirling,
In the depth of endless night.

Comets trace their stories,
In arcs against the dark.
Each flicker is a message,
A distant shining spark.

Planets hum in silence,
Their orbits never cease.
In the vast celestial dance,
We find a sense of peace.

The Echoing Heart

Within the chest of silence,
A heart begins to beat.
With every pulse, a rhythm,
In solitude, we meet.

Whispers of our longing,
Rippling through the void.
In the depth of our being,
Our dreams are not destroyed.

Time moves like a shadow,
Fleeting yet so near.
In echoes of our heartbeat,
Our truths become so clear.

Beneath the stars above us,
Hope dances in the dark.
In every fragile heartbeat,
Lies the fire, the spark.

Cadence of the Celestial Slate

Stars whisper secrets in the night,
Galaxies twirl in a cosmic flight.
Moonlight dances on the quiet waves,
Time stands still, as the darkness saves.

Comets trace paths through the endless blue,
Each flicker a wish, a dream come true.
Nebulas bloom in colors so bright,
Painting the canvas of endless night.

The universe sings with a gentle hum,
In harmony, all the constellations come.
A rhythm of light, a celestial beat,
In this grand symphony, we find our seat.

Embrace the wonder, let your heart soar,
For in the heavens, there's always more.
With each twinkle, our spirits unite,
In the cadence of stars, we find our light.

The Gentle Weight of Earth's Embrace

Beneath the trees, where shadows play,
The soil whispers secrets of the day.
Roots entwined in a loving grasp,
Nature's chorus, a tender clasp.

Mountains stand guard, their majesty known,
Fields of green, where wildflowers have grown.
The soft touch of grass beneath our feet,
A sanctuary where heartbeats meet.

Rivers weave tales through valleys wide,
In their currents, the memories glide.
Each pebble tells stories of ages past,
In Earth's embrace, we find peace at last.

Listen closely to the earth's soft sigh,
In each breeze, hear the lullaby.
With gentle weight, our souls intertwine,
In nature's arms, we are forever fine.

Timeless Voices in the Geode

Within the rock, a hidden glow,
Whispers of time in a crystal show.
Silent treasures, nature's art,
In each layer, a beating heart.

Echoes of age in every line,
Stardust memories, divine design.
Ridges and valleys, each facet bright,
Holding the shadows of ancient light.

As you crack it open, hear the chime,
Of stories woven through the fabric of time.
Each voice a gem, each thought a sound,
In the geode's heart, magic is found.

Open your mind to the tales they share,
Timeless voices linger in the air.
With the wisdom of ages, they create,
A symphony of love that won't abate.

Lucent Stones, Luminescent Dreams

On the shore where the waves kiss the sand,
Stones glimmer softly, like a lover's hand.
Moonlight drapes the beach in silk,
As dreams flow in like warm, sweet milk.

Each stone a story, a whispering light,
Echoes of journeys through day and night.
They shimmer and shine with a secret gleam,
Guardians of hope, where we dare to dream.

In twilight's glow, they begin to hum,
Voices of the earth in the soft, sweet strum.
A tapestry woven of wish and flight,
Guided by stars, in the gentle night.

Embrace the magic, let your spirit soar,
With lucent stones, we seek for more.
In the realm of dreams, and echoing streams,
Together we wander, crafting our schemes.

Eternal Whispers of Weathered Walls

Time whispers through the aged stone,
Secrets echo, soft and lone.
Tales of laughter, tales of pain,
In every crack, memories remain.

Moss-clad shadows dance in light,
Sheltering dreams within the night.
A breeze carries stories untold,
Into the heart, both young and old.

With each raindrop, the walls sigh,
A lullaby of the earth and sky.
They hold the weight of years gone by,
Where echoes linger, never die.

Weathered and worn, they stand so tall,
Guardians of history, they enthrall.
In silence, they weave their steady call,
Eternal whispers of weathered walls.

The Embrace of Mellow Marble

Polished silhouettes embrace the light,
Veins of nature, pure delight.
Each curve tells a story dear,
In the hush, I find you here.

Warmth radiates from every stone,
In every grain, I feel at home.
Soft whispers of an artist's hand,
Mellow marble, forever grand.

Glistening beneath the sun's warm glow,
A gentle touch in the ebb and flow.
Here, time drifts like a silent tide,
In this embrace, I shall abide.

Ancient dreams in hues divine,
With every layer, stories entwine.
Together, in this sacred space,
We find a love in marble's grace.

Inscriptions of Inner Calm

Beneath the chaos, a stillness breathes,
In every moment, solace weaves.
Quiet thoughts as shadows play,
They guide the heart, they light the way.

Inscriptions carved in fading light,
A tranquil pause, a quiet night.
Whispers of wisdom softly call,
To seek the peace within it all.

Ripples dance on a silver stream,
Reflections of a waking dream.
Gentle waves cradle the mind,
In stillness, a truth we find.

The heartbeats echo, soft and warm,
In the silence, we feel the balm.
Embrace the glow of quiet grace,
Inscriptions of calm, a sacred space.

A Tonic in the Texture of Terrain

Rugged hills and valleys deep,
A tonic where the wild things leap.
Between the blades of grass so fine,
Nature's sketch in every line.

Windswept whispers brush the ground,
In every layer, life is found.
The earth hums its ancient song,
In the texture, we all belong.

Stones tell tales of years gone by,
Beneath the vast and open sky.
Each fold and crease, a memory,
A living archive, wild and free.

Here in the rugged, beauty reigns,
A tonic flows through our veins.
With every step on this rich terrain,
We dance in the rhythm of nature's gain.

Ageless Echoes of Tranquil Stone

In whispering winds they lie,
Ancient tales of earth and sky,
Each stone a bearer of time's weight,
Silent witness, patient fate.

Moss-clad giants stand so tall,
Guardians of the forest's call,
Their presence calms the restless mind,
In their shadows, peace we find.

With every step on sacred ground,
The echoing past is profound,
Nature's voice, a soft refrain,
In tranquil moments, we remain.

Through ages past, the stones persist,
In gentle light, they co-exist,
An ageless dance of love and grace,
In quietude, we find our place.

The Resonance of Earthly Wonders

Mountains rise with prideful grace,
Veils of mist that softly trace,
Nature's symphony plays loud,
In the wild, we stand unbowed.

Rivers sing their ancient song,
Flowing where the heart belongs,
Each ripple tells a story fair,
Of the journey, bold and rare.

Forests hum with whispered lore,
Leaves that dance and spirits soar,
In every branch, a tale retold,
Of earthly wonders, brave and bold.

Skies ignite in colors bright,
Blankets soft with stars at night,
Nature's canvas, vast and wide,
In her embrace, we take pride.

The Calm Chorus of the Canyons

Echoes flutter through the stone,
Notes of nature, softly grown,
In the depths, a tranquil sound,
Where whispers of the past abound.

Breezes carry tales of old,
Carved in rock, a story bold,
Time-worn crevices applaud,
In stillness, silence feels like God.

Sunlight dances on the walls,
Shadowed twilight gently falls,
In between the highs and lows,
The canyon's heart forever glows.

With every breath, we find our peace,
In this calm, our worries cease,
Nature's chorus, pure and bright,
Guiding souls through day and night.

Celestial Bodies, Earthly Echoes

Stars are scattered, dreams ignite,
Across the vast and endless night,
In their glow, our fantasies soar,
Into the cosmos, we explore.

Planets dance with silent grace,
In the heavens, we find our place,
Yet on the ground, our roots go deep,
In earthy echoes, secrets sleep.

Galaxies whisper, tales of old,
In stardust, vivid and bold,
Yet here, beneath the sky's embrace,
We forge connections, find our space.

Celestial bodies, guides above,
But earthly echoes, warm with love,
In every heartbeat, we align,
In the universe, our souls entwine.

Foundations of Tranquility

In the soft shadows of dawn's embrace,
Gentle whispers weave through the trees.
Stillness settles like a warm grace,
Nature's song drifts on the breeze.

Quiet waters reflect the skies,
Mirrored secrets from the deep.
Birds on branches softly sigh,
Peaceful moments, ours to keep.

A rustle, a movement in the air,
Leaves dance lightly, shadows play.
Tranquil hearts, free from care,
Find solace in the break of day.

Every breath a tender sigh,
Crickets hum a lulling tune.
Underneath the vast expanse,
We fold ourselves into the afternoon.

Unyielding Grace in Mineral Light

Beneath the weight of ancient stone,
Silent strength in every crack.
Time washes over, yet alone,
These formations hold no lack.

Sunlight dances on rough edges,
Casting shadows rich and bright.
Nature's canvas, with no ledges,
Holds the balance of the night.

Mountains whisper tales of yore,
Each layer tells a different tale.
In stillness, they forever bore,
A legacy that will not pale.

Grace within the hardened face,
Timeless beauty that won't fade.
In their presence, we find space,
To ponder all that's never made.

Conversations Between Pebbles

In the quiet of a sunlit glade,
Pebbles chat beneath the sky.
Colors speaking, stories laid,
In their stillness, they comply.

A smooth stone tells of rivers run,
While jagged edges share the fight.
With laughter, they recount the sun,
Sharing glimmers of delight.

Each a witness to time's embrace,
Held by earth, yet bold and free.
Their whispers shift in gentle grace,
Rooted deep in harmony.

Together they form paths anew,
Underneath the grassy sweep.
In simplicity, wisdom grew,
From conversations softly steeped.

The Still Choir of Mountains

High above, the peaks stand proud,
Quiet sentinels in the night.
Echoes of their song, unbowed,
Sing in whispers, calm and light.

Snow-capped crowns kiss azure skies,
Their solemn beauty speaks in hymns.
Nature listens, earth complies,
In this silence, spirit swims.

Every ridge, a voice so clear,
In the stillness, power swells.
With each glance, we draw near,
To the secrets that silence tells.

Together they hold steady ground,
A choir without a defined place.
In their stillness, glory found,
Mountains reign with timeless grace.

The Contours of Contentment

In quiet nooks, the shadows play,
Where whispers weave through golden hay.
The sun dips low, a gentle sigh,
In the arms of dusk, dreams softly lie.

A brook hums sweet, its secrets share,
While wildflowers nod with fragrant air.
Each moment savored, time holds still,
Contentment flows like water, will.

With every breeze, the world feels right,
Colors blend in the fading light.
In simple joys, hearts find their home,
Embracing peace, no need to roam.

Under the stars, the night unfolds,
As stories told by firelight molds.
In every pulse, the soul's delight,
The contours of joy in the gentle night.

Patterns of Harmony in the Henge

Stones stand tall where time has waned,
Echoes of laughter softly gained.
In circles drawn, the past holds sway,
Where ancient whispers guide the sway.

Patterns etched in the earth below,
Mark the rhythm of the sun's glow.
Each stone a note in nature's song,
Resonating where we all belong.

The moonlight dances on rugged ground,
In the stillness, lost dreams are found.
With every breath, the earth aligns,
In sacred shapes, a truth defines.

The henge, a keeper of the lore,
Where harmony blooms forevermore.
In sacred silence, hearts expand,
United by the magic of the land.

The Graces of Gneiss and Granite

Rugged cliffs kissed by morning light,
Tell tales of strength, a wondrous sight.
Layers of history, natures art,
In gneiss and granite, life's deep heart.

With every crack, a story unfolds,
In hues of gray, deep greens and golds.
Time's gentle hands have shaped the stone,
Each grain a whisper of the unknown.

Mountains rise where eagles soar,
Guardians at nature's timeless door.
In their embrace, one finds their place,
A rocky ode to earth's embrace.

Amidst the peaks, the spirit lifts,
In silent reverence, the heart sifts.
The graces held in stone's strong hand,
Speak of endurance across the land.

Odes to the Hidden Heart of Rock

Deep within the layers dark,
Lies the essence, the sacred spark.
Beneath the surface, secrets dwell,
In the heart of rock, stories swell.

Each chisel strike reveals the core,
An ancient language, forever more.
From every fissure, a tale breaks free,
Whispers of time, soft as the sea.

Crystals shimmer in the gentle light,
A universe within, pure and bright.
In every heartbeat, the earth's deep song,
A symphony of ages, pure and strong.

A lasting ode to what lies beneath,
In silent strength, the earth bequeath.
Odes to the hidden, strong and grand,
In the heart of rock, life's steady hand.

Quietude on the Path of Pebbles

Gentle whispers in the breeze,
Footfalls dance on quiet stones.
The sun dips low, the shadows tease,
Each moment stands, yet time postpones.

A soft sigh from trees above,
The heart finds space to simply breathe.
A feeling both tender and of love,
In this calm, my soul believes.

Pebbles tell stories of the past,
Every step a tale unfurls.
Nature's peace, a spell so vast,
In silence, life's rhythm swirls.

Pause awhile, let worries cease,
In quietude, the spirit mends.
Where nature holds a sweet release,
On this path, my journey bends.

Nature's Harmonious Composition

In the forest, a songbird sings,
Leaves shimmer in the morning light.
The wind caresses, softly brings,
A chorus of life, pure delight.

Rivers flow with joyous laughter,
Mountains stand in silent grace.
Every moment leads to after,
In nature's arms, I find my place.

Sunset's glow paints skies so bright,
Colors blend in perfect form.
Stars awaken in the night,
A world transformed, a calming warm.

Harmony in every sound,
Insects hum, and trees sway low.
Nature's beauty all around,
In this peace, my heart will grow.

Reverie in the Rough Edges

Jagged cliffs and waves that crash,
Nature's fury, fierce and bold.
Yet in chaos, dreams still flash,
A beauty in the wild unfolds.

Clouds unravel, twisting high,
Sky and sea in wild embrace.
In the storm, I long to fly,
To find myself in nature's grace.

Craggy paths where few have trod,
Soulful whispers in the air.
Amongst the rough, I feel the prod,
Of quiet hopes, devoid of care.

Here in the shadows, light can peek,
In every flaw, a story blooms.
In rough edges, solace speak,
Where heart and spirit find their rooms.

Feelings Etched in Stone

Time etches tales upon the rocks,
Whispers of those who came before.
In silence, memory unlocks,
Captured moments we can't ignore.

Underneath the aged boughs,
Written in the grains of sand.
Feelings rise, as time allows,
Each impression, softly planned.

A heart's echo in every crack,
Nature's pen, it sculpts and shapes.
No need for words, no looking back,
In stone, the essence gently drapes.

Beneath the skies of twilight's hue,
Reflections drown in tranquil pools.
Feelings, timeless, simple, true,
In nature's arms, the spirit cools.

Landscapes of Agreement

In fields where harmony blooms,
Soft whispers dance among the trees,
The sun and shadows weave bright tapestries,
A canvas rich, where purpose looms.

Rivers flow with gentle grace,
Reflecting peace upon their skin,
Mountains stand, both proud and wise,
Nature's heart, a steady place.

Birds sing anthems in the air,
While flowers nod, agreeing too,
In unity, the world stands tall,
Embracing life, a love affair.

Together, hand in hand we roam,
In landscapes lush, where souls align,
With every step, we find our way,
In agreed paths, we find our home.

The Symphony of Stillness

In quiet woods where echoes fade,
A symphony of silence plays,
Trees sway gently, their secret tunes,
A world embraced in softest shade.

The hush of night blankets the land,
Stars twinkle in a serene dance,
Moonlight casts its silver glow,
In stillness, we find nature's hand.

Each breath a note, a tender sigh,
Whispers of wind in the branches high,
A melody that fills the heart,
In every pause, our spirits fly.

Together, we linger, side by side,
In this grand orchestra of calm,
Finding solace in the night,
In stillness, we let love abide.

Nature's Soft Conversations

In meadows bright, the daisies speak,
With petals soft as whispered dreams,
Breezes carry their gentle words,
Nature's voice in quiet streaks.

The brook hums low, a soothing tune,
While leaves applaud in cheerful dance,
A language spoken without sound,
In every moment, life attunes.

Clouds drift lazily, sharing sighs,
Their shadows brush the land below,
As sunbeams join in, warm and bright,
In nature's chat, time softly flies.

Together, we watch this ballet unfold,
In soft conversations, hearts awaken,
Finding peace in blooms and sighs,
In the language of love, we are consoled.

Channels of Unity

In rivers wide, we find our flow,
Where waters weave through earth and stone,
Connecting shores, both far and near,
In channels deep, our spirits grow.

Mountains rise, their peaks embrace,
The clouds above, in drift and chase,
A summit reached, where whispers blend,
In nature's arms, we find our space.

Each path we tread, a thread of fate,
Bridges built by hands of time,
In unity, we walk as one,
With open hearts, we celebrate.

Together, we venture with open minds,
In channels rich, where hopes ignite,
With every step, the world's a song,
In unity, our spirits bind.

Breath of the Boulders

Whispers of stone in the breeze,
Echoes of time, gentle and free.
Cracked faces wear stories untold,
In shadows of giants, the air feels old.

Moss carpets soft on gray skin,
A silent embrace where life has been.
Roots intertwine deep in the earth,
As boulders cradle the secrets of birth.

Each rise and fall, under the stars,
Marks out the rhythm of ancient wars.
Weathered hands reach out in grace,
Holding the tales of nature's embrace.

In twilight hues, they stand alive,
With every pulse, the earth does thrive.
Breath of the boulders, an ageless song,
In every heartbeat, where we belong.

The Stillness Beneath the Surface

Beneath the lake, a whispering pause,
Hidden depths without a cause.
Rippling dreams that colors weave,
In the silence, shadows believe.

The water holds a sleeping grace,
In its depths, time finds its space.
Fishes dart like thoughts unfurl,
In the stillness, the world's a pearl.

Stone and sand in quiet play,
Guard the secrets of night and day.
What lies below, still and profound,
Calls to the heart with a muted sound.

The surface shimmers, a delicate guise,
Concealing magic beneath the skies.
The stillness breathes, a gentle sigh,
In its embrace, the mysteries lie.

The Tranquil Architecture of Rock

Stone towers rise with quiet might,
In their presence, the day feels bright.
Nature's artistry, bold and free,
In every curve, a harmony.

Layers tell tales of ages past,
Crafted by time, built to last.
Sunlight dances on rugged walls,
In this structure, a calmness calls.

Stalactites hang like dreams in flight,
While shadows weave with soft moonlight.
Arching bridges, the silent hymn,
In the heart of the earth, life begins.

These ancient forms, a sacred space,
Hold the wisdom of time's embrace.
The tranquil rock, a silent guide,
In its presence, we abide.

Meditations in Limestone

In caverns deep, the coolness breathes,
Limestone dreams weave through the leaves.
Whispers of water carve their song,
In the dark, where shadows belong.

A tapestry of light and shade,
Where the memories of earth have laid.
Columns rise with grace, sublime,
Holding a moment outside of time.

Each echo flows like a gentle stream,
In the silence, reality gleams.
Fragments of peace, cradled tight,
Meditations in the soft, dim light.

Stone reflections embrace the mind,
In the stillness, clarity we find.
Limestone whispers the world's refrain,
In its presence, we feel no pain.

Songs of the Stalwart Stones

Beneath the weight of centuries,
A chorus soft, yet profound,
Rumbling echoes through the ages,
In silence, wisdom is found.

Mighty boulders stand unwavering,
Guardians of the earth's own heart,
While whispers dance upon the breezes,
Stories told that won't depart.

Each crack a tale of thunder,
Each shadow a history's grace,
The stones hum songs of steadfastness,
In nature's unyielding embrace.

So let us journey to their voices,
Listen closely to their tone,
In the timeless songs of the stalwart,
We discover we are not alone.

Elysian Fields of Uncut Gemstones

In valleys lush with hidden treasures,
Sparkling lights in nature's care,
Flashes of uncut brilliance,
Glisten softly, rare and fair.

Amidst the green, their colors whisper,
Each facet tells of time's sweet grace,
A tapestry of living jewels,
Adorning earth, a grand embrace.

In Elysium's quiet laughter,
With sunlit beams that gently gleam,
They cradle dreams of ancient wisdom,
Casting hearts in tranquil dream.

Beneath the skies of endless beauty,
These gemstones, pure, will ever shine,
In this enchanted land of wonder,
We find our souls in every line.

The Lullaby of Ancient Cliff Faces

Whispers ride the ocean's breezes,
Cradled in the cliffside strong,
Ancient faces, weathered gently,
Singing nature's timeless song.

Each line engraved by wind's caress,
Stories of the tides they bear,
In shadows cast by setting sunlight,
Secrets linger in the air.

With every wave, their lullabies,
Soothing hearts who pause to see,
Eternal truths on steep horizons,
Lessons learned from land and sea.

Let us listen to their murmurs,
Find solace in the stone's embrace,
For in the lullaby of ancients,
We uncover time and space.

Tides of Stillness on Stony Shores

Waves retreat with gentle murmur,
Softly kiss the weathered land,
On stony shores, the stillness lingers,
Time flows like fine, golden sand.

Pebbles dance in rhythmic patterns,
Each a tale of ancient tides,
In the hush of nature's cradle,
Peaceful beauty softly hides.

The sea's deep breaths, a calming presence,
Where troubles vanish, fade away,
In the tides of tranquil stillness,
We find the strength for our day.

On shores where silence wraps the stones,
We breathe in memories of the deep,
In the dance of time, forever flowing,
The stony shores invite our sleep.

Whispers of Granite

Beneath the sun's warm gaze, it stands,
Silent sentinel of time and land.
Weathered edges, stories unfold,
In whispers soft, the rocks grow old.

Moss blankets stones, a gentle cloak,
Nature's breath in every stroke.
Echoes linger in the mountain's heart,
A sanctuary where shadows part.

Cracks and crevices, secrets hide,
In every fissure, the past resides.
A canvas where the ages play,
In the twilight's glow, they softly sway.

Granite tales of the earth they share,
A symphony woven in the air.
Listen closely, and you might find,
The wisdom of ages, intertwined.

Echoes of Earth

Beneath the sky, the earth does sigh,
Through valleys deep, where shadows lie.
Whispers rise from the soil's core,
Echoes of life, forevermore.

Mountains stand with a regal grace,
Each peak a memory, time can't erase.
Rivers carve their timeless song,
In nature's arms, we all belong.

The dance of leaves in the breeze's sweep,
Secrets within, the earth does keep.
Tales of growth in each gentle sway,
Resonating softly, night and day.

Voices in stone and soil combined,
A symphony for the heart and mind.
Listen closely, the earth will teach,
In its embrace, all souls reach.

Symphonic Silhouettes

In twilight's glow, they start to rise,
Shapes emerging in the evening skies.
Mountains play a silent tune,
Symphonic silhouettes 'neath the moon.

Shadows dance in the fading light,
Beneath the stars that shine so bright.
Each contour tells a story bold,
Of journeys past, in whispers told.

Winds weave through the craggy heights,
A melody of ancient sights.
Echoes of life, both soft and strong,
With every breath, they sing their song.

The night unfolds its vast embrace,
As time takes on a slower pace.
In harmony, the earth confides,
In symphonic silhouettes, it hides.

Songs of the Ancient Rock

Deep in the hills where silence sings,
Lies a rock with forgotten wings.
Cradling echoes of days gone by,
Songs of the earth that never die.

Worn by the hands of grazing time,
In every crack, a rhythm, a rhyme.
The ancient tales in the twilight glow,
Whispered softly, a sacred flow.

Roots entwined in the sacred ground,
In every heartbeat, a pulse profound.
Beneath the starlit, endless sky,
Songs of the rock rise softly, nigh.

Age-old rhythms swirl in the breeze,
Swaying softly through towering trees.
Nature's chorus, a timeless call,
In songs of the ancient rock, we fall.

Solace in the Stone's Song

In the quiet whispers of the stone,
Ancient echoes call me home.
Each pebble holds a tale untold,
A melody of time, silent yet bold.

Beneath the weight of weary years,
Soft murmurings soothe my fears.
I find my peace in shadows cast,
As the world around me drifts so fast.

The river's flow sings through my heart,
In nature's choir, I play my part.
Every grain of sand, every towering tree,
In the stone's song, I find my plea.

Harmony found in sacred ground,
In the stillness, love is profound.
I linger here, my spirit drawn,
In the embrace of the stone's song at dawn.

The Winding Path of Resilience

Through valleys deep and mountains high,
I wander where the wild winds sigh.
Each step a lesson, a stumble, a rise,
The winding path opens my eyes.

Roots dig deep in varied soil,
Struggles shaped by time and toil.
With every turn, a story blooms,
In the dance of life, the heart consumes.

Though the storms may come and go,
In every shadow, there's a glow.
Resilience weaves a strong embrace,
Guiding me through the toughest place.

With every breath, I find my way,
The sun will rise, it's here to stay.
In the journey's end, I stand so tall,
On this winding path, I've conquered all.

A Canvas of Coquina

On the shore where dreams are spun,
A canvas of coquina, golden run.
Each shell a whisper from the sea,
Stories woven in harmony.

Windbrush strokes through grains of sand,
Nature's palette, beautifully planned.
Wave after wave, they paint and clash,
Creating art in an endless splash.

A tapestry of colors, soft and bright,
In the morning sun, a wondrous sight.
Every tide brings a new design,
Each moment fleeting, divine, benign.

Here I stand, enraptured by grace,
Lost in the beauty of this place.
A canvas of coquina, wild and free,
A masterpiece, forever a part of me.

Layers of Love in the Loam

In the earthy depths where secrets lie,
Layers of love beneath the sky.
Fertile soil holds dreams anew,
Nurtured by the heart's sweet dew.

Roots entwined in a tender embrace,
Life flourishes in this sacred space.
From dark to light, it weaves a thread,
In the loam of love, we are led.

Each season brings a gentle change,
In the garden's heart, we rearrange.
Blossoms born from patience and care,
Layers of love, a bond we share.

As time unfurls, we grow more wise,
In the loam's richness, our spirits rise.
Here I find my joy and peace,
In layers of love, life finds release.

The Solidity of Silk-Stone Dreams

In the quiet dawn of gentle light,
Silk-stone dreams take fearless flight.
Whispers of hope in pastel hues,
Crafting a world where love renews.

With every thread of stitched desire,
They weave a truth that won't expire.
A tapestry of thoughts embraced,
In the heart's fabric softly traced.

Beneath the stars, these dreams entwined,
Carved from stone, yet gentle, kind.
Each shimmer tells a story bold,
In night's embrace, their tales unfold.

So hold these dreams, let them inspire,
A silk-stone path through worlds entire.
For in the heart, their essence gleams,
In the silence, we find our dreams.

The Alchemy of Nature's Palette

Nature's brush strokes, wild and free,
Paint the canvas of you and me.
Emerald greens and azure skies,
Each hue a truth that never lies.

Golden sunsets, vibrant and warm,
Nature's beauty is a sacred form.
Through every season's dance and sway,
The palette shifts in wondrous play.

From winter's white to summer's gold,
Each color whispers stories told.
In rainbows bright, or shadows deep,
Nature's art awakens sleep.

So let us journey hand in hand,
Through fields of colors, wild and grand.
For in each shade, a spark ignites,
The alchemy of our shared delights.

Portraits of Peace in the Pebbled Path

Down the pebbled path we roam,
Each stone a story, each step a home.
Portraits of peace in every glance,
Stitching moments into a dance.

The soft crunch echoes calm and clear,
Whispers of nature, serenity near.
In the sunlight, shadows play,
Guiding us gently on our way.

As we wander through time's embrace,
Finding solace in nature's grace.
Each pebble laid with intention true,
Holds a reflection of me and you.

So let us treasure this sacred ground,
In the silence, let love abound.
For in every step we softly take,
We find the peace that dreams awake.

Songs of Solidarity in the Stony Pasture

In the stony pasture, we unite,
Voices rising, bold and bright.
Songs of solidarity we sing,
In harmony, our spirits spring.

With every note, a heart laid bare,
We craft a melody of care.
In the rustling grass, the wind takes flight,
Carrying dreams into the night.

Together we stand on this rugged land,
Sowing hope with a steadfast hand.
In the face of storms, we remain strong,
Bound by the rhythm of our song.

So let the music echo wide,
In every heart, let love reside.
For in this pasture, side by side,
We sow the seeds of hope and pride.

The Melody of Timeworn Rocks

Whispers of ages hide in stone,
Echoes of tales not fully known.
Veins of history beneath the crust,
Silent witnesses, unyielding dust.

Time has carved each crevice deep,
In shadows where the dark secrets sleep.
Moss will dance upon their face,
Nature's soft, embracing grace.

The wind will hum a gentle tune,
As day gives way to the silver moon.
In every rock, a story breathes,
A memory that the silence weaves.

Together, they stand in quiet pride,
Bearing witness to life's wild ride.
In each crack and curve, wisdom flows,
A melody of time, forever glows.

Chisel and Caress: A Sculptor's Tale

With chisel in hand, a vision blooms,
Beneath the dust, the marble looms.
Each strike a heartbeat, each chip a sigh,
A dance of creation beneath the sky.

The sculptor's eye sees not just stone,
But lives within each curve, alone.
With gentle caress, the shape reveals,
A story shared, a fate that heals.

Fingers trace where art begins,
Forming beauty from the sins.
As dust settles on the floor,
A masterpiece opens its door.

In the quiet, the marble sings,
Of love and loss and all life brings.
A tale of hope, of dreams set free,
In every form, eternity.

Symphony Beneath the Surface

Beneath the waves, a silence lingers,
An orchestra played by unseen fingers.
Currents flow with stories untold,
A ballet of life in textures bold.

Fish weave through coral, vibrant and bright,
Swaying gently in soft twilight.
In swirling schools, they dance with glee,
Echoes of laughter, wild and free.

In the depths, the shadows play,
A symphony crafted in a secret way.
Whales sing songs of love and loss,
A journey etched with every toss.

The ocean breathes a timeless sound,
Its heartbeats rhythmical, profound.
In depths where curiosity roams,
A symphony waits, calling us home.

Stillness in the Stone Garden

In the garden where silence reigns,
Stone statues guard the earthly lanes.
Each figure, still, yet full of grace,
A tranquil time in this sacred space.

Moss creeps slowly over the years,
Whispering secrets, calming fears.
Sunlight dapples on weathered stone,
An embrace from a world unknown.

The breeze carries tales of the past,
Fleeting moments, forever cast.
In circles 'round the ancient trees,
Nature's breath is felt among the leaves.

Chimes of peace, a gentle call,
Inviting stillness to one and all.
In this garden, hearts find home,
Where stone and spirit freely roam.

Reflections of Peace in Petrified Dreams

In silent woods where shadows fall,
The whispers of the ancients call.
Beneath the bark, the stories sleep,
In dreams of stone, our souls we keep.

Moonlit paths through ages pine,
With echoes sweet, our hearts align.
Each leaf a page of timeless lore,
In petrified breaths, forevermore.

Stillness reigns in twilight's glow,
The roots of time, they softly flow.
In every grain, a tale unfolds,
Of peace and love and dreams retold.

As stars ignite the shadowed sky,
The world transforms, and we comply.
In this embrace, we find our way,
Through petrified dreams, in peace we stay.

The Artistry of Lithic Love

Carved by time, the stones embrace,
Each rugged line a tender trace.
In silent beauty, they declare,
The love that blooms beyond compare.

Across the land, these sculptures stand,
Chiseled hearts in nature's hand.
With every crack, a story speaks,
Of passion found in mountain peaks.

The colors dance in sunlight's grace,
A testament to time and space.
In every crevice, shadows play,
Artistry of love in stone's array.

From geode's core to river's bend,
Life's sculpted love will never end.
In the artistry of lithic dreams,
Our hearts, like stones, find perfect seams.

Tuning Forks of the Earth

The mountains hum a steady tune,
In harmony with sun and moon.
Resonance flows through every stone,
Creating chords that feel like home.

With every quake, the earth aligns,
In silent songs, the world entwines.
Tuning forks of ancient ground,
In symphonies of peace, we're found.

The rivers sing, the valleys sigh,
As nature's choir fills the sky.
In whispered notes, our hearts will soar,
To join the earth's eternal score.

Together we will find our place,
In rhythms woven with a grace.
The tuning forks of life, they share,
A melody beyond compare.

Celestial Chords in Basalt

Beneath the stars, the basalt dreams,
In shadowed forms, celestial beams.
Each crack within, a song discreet,
The universe in heartbeats sweet.

A cosmic dance of rock and light,
Echoing softly through the night.
In every stone, a tale is spun,
Of galaxies, and life begun.

As stardust falls on ancient stone,
A symphony of love is grown.
In solitude, we feel the spark,
Of cosmic chords in every dark.

Together, lost in night's embrace,
We find our peace, our sacred space.
Celestial chords will lead us near,
In basalt dreams, our hearts adhere.

Dreams in the Dust

In the quiet corners lay,
Whispers of a fading day.
Silent hopes in shadows blend,
Where the broken dreams descend.

Footprints left upon the ground,
Echoes lost, yet still they sound.
Dusty trails of what once was,
Linger softly, just because.

With a breath, the past can sigh,
In the twilight's gentle eye.
Moments caught like fleeting rays,
In the dust, the heart still plays.

So we chase, in twilight's glow,
Dreams that shimmer, ebb, and flow.
Though the paths may soon go bare,
Hope remains, forever there.

The Stillness of Ages

Time stands still beneath the trees,
Whispers lost in the soft breeze.
Branches arch like ancient tales,
Carried forth by distant gales.

On the ground, the leaves decay,
Yet stories linger, fade away.
In the hush, a heartbeat sounds,
Resonates through sacred grounds.

Eons pass without a fight,
In the dark, there lies a light.
Fleeting moments, woven tight,
In stillness, wisdom takes its flight.

A dance of stars, a cosmic thread,
All that's spoken, all that's said.
In the silence, voices merge,
A timeless call, a soft surge.

Confluence of the Crags

Where the mountains kiss the sky,
Rivers rush, and echoes cry.
Stony giants stand so tall,
Guarding secrets, one and all.

In their depths, the shadows play,
Sunlight gleams, then slips away.
Water weaves through rock and time,
A melody, a whispered rhyme.

Nature's hands sculpt every line,
Rugged edges, pure design.
At the crags where paths align,
Hearts converge in sacred sign.

Here, the spirit comes alive,
In this place, we learn to thrive.
With each step, the journey grows,
In the crags, the wild wind blows.

The Art of Enduring

Through the storms, we hold our ground,
Roots entwined, forever bound.
In the quiet, strength is found,
In the silence, truth profound.

Time can wear away the stone,
Yet we stand, not all alone.
With each scar, a story made,
In life's canvas, colors laid.

From the falls, we rise anew,
With each dawn, we see the view.
Hope rekindles, bright and pure,
In the heart, a steadfast cure.

Though the path may twist and bend,
We will brave until the end.
In the struggle, beauty sings,
In enduring, our spirit springs.

The Calm of Kaleidoscopic Minerals

In shades of blue and green, they lay,
Fragments of Earth in bright array.
Each piece whispers a silent tale,
Of time and beauty in a grand scale.

Their colors shift with the light's embrace,
A dance of hues, a gentle grace.
In nature's hand, a soothing balm,
These minerals bring a heartful calm.

With every glance, a new view found,
In the calmness, there's a soft sound.
They cradle dreams in vibrant hues,
Kaleidoscopic love in nature's clues.

Together they form a stunning sight,
A tapestry rich, a pure delight.
In every facet, a world anew,
In minerals' calm, we find our truth.

Veins of Unity in Stone Veil

Below the surface, layers blend,
A hidden world that has no end.
Veins of unity, in stone concealed,
Silent stories, the Earth has healed.

Each crack a path, each line a trace,
Whispers of time in this quiet space.
Together they stand, strong and fine,
In stony hearts, our spirits shine.

Connections form, where life can thrive,
In the depths, we feel alive.
Through ancient rocks, we sense the call,
Veins of unity, embracing all.

In this stone veil, we find our root,
Grounded deep, our souls take suit.
Together we rise, together we'll grow,
In the veins of Earth, unity flows.

A Tapestry Woven in Quartz and Clay

Within the earth, a mix so rare,
Quartz and clay knit with care.
A tapestry formed in nature's loom,
Underneath the sun's warm bloom.

Textures blend in a dance divine,
Crafting beauty, intertwining lines.
With every layer, a story unfolds,
Of ancient times and treasures untold.

Each thread a journey, each hue a dream,
Together they whisper, together they beam.
In quartz's sparkle, in clay's rich earth,
We discover the essence of rebirth.

Woven gently, like time's embrace,
A tapestry bright in this sacred place.
In unity, these elements play,
A legacy born from quartz and clay.

Echoing Souls Beneath the Surface

Beneath the crust, where shadows rest,
Echoing souls in silence blessed.
Whispers of ages, faint yet clear,
In the depths, our hearts draw near.

Translucent dreams in cavern sleep,
Unfurling stories, secrets to keep.
With every echo, a memory blooms,
Of life entwined in forgotten tombs.

In the stillness, we feel their grace,
A gentle touch in this hidden place.
Echoing souls in harmony sway,
Beneath the surface, they softly play.

Together they sing, a haunting choir,
Filling the void with our deepest desire.
In the earth's embrace, we find our birth,
Echoing souls, the heart of Earth.

Echoing Valleys

In the shadows of the hills,
Whispers dance on gentle breeze.
Songs of nature, sweetly thrill,
Each echo brings the heart at ease.

Clouds drift softly overhead,
Waves of green embrace the ground.
In this realm, no tears to shed,
Harmony in every sound.

Rivers carve their ancient tales,
Over rocks so worn and wise.
Through these paths, the spirit sails,
Beneath an ever-changing sky.

Hills respond to every call,
Nature's choir, pure and true.
In this land, we stand in thrall,
Echoes bind me close to you.

Silent Pinnacles

Majestic peaks against the blue,
Guardians of the silent hour.
In their shade, the quiet grew,
Nature's strength, a timeless power.

Flakes of snow like whispered dreams,
Adorning heights with perfect grace.
In their stillness, morning beams,
A tranquil heart finds its safe place.

Starlit nights upon their crowns,
Glimmers of a far-off past.
Winds carry ancient, solemn sounds,
By their grace, the die is cast.

Climb the heights, let worries cease,
Feel the calm in every breath.
In their majesty, find peace,
Silent pinnacles embrace our death.

Tones of Time in Terracotta

Clay and earth beneath our feet,
Molds of ages long gone by.
Each shard holds a story sweet,
Whispers of the earth, a sigh.

Colors blend in muted hues,
Echoing the hands that shaped.
In this art, the heart renews,
Life's tapestry, forever draped.

Through the kiln, the magic flows,
Fires ignite what once was still.
In every crack, a journey shows,
Life's rhythms shape the spirit's will.

Terracotta warms the night,
An embrace of time's soft glow.
In its presence, find the light,
Crafted from all we strive to know.

Stone-Sculpted Serenity

In the quiet, silence breathes,
Stones that hum of years gone past.
Beneath the weight, a strength weaves,
Echoes of peace, forever cast.

Carved by hands, a loving grace,
Figures emerge from muted rock.
In their stillness, time's embrace,
A gentle tick, a steady clock.

Granite faces guard the land,
Weathered tales in every line.
In this realm, we understand,
Nature and art so intertwine.

Beneath the starlit, velvet sky,
Stone embraces the evening star.
In this bond, we sigh and fly,
Finding solace, near and far.

Tapestry of Earth's Patience

Every grain, a tale untold,
Woven through the tapestry.
Patience is the earth's pure gold,
In its layers, we find the key.

Mountains rise, and rivers flow,
Patterns etched in time's embrace.
In this dance, we feel the glow,
Life's rhythm in nature's grace.

Fields of green stretch infinitely,
Each bloom speaks of love and care.
In the silence, we agree,
Earth holds treasures we all share.

With every step upon this ground,
Breathe the wisdom of the wise.
In this beauty, peace is found,
Tapestry beneath the skies.

Lines of the Lamented

In the shadows, whispers fade,
Memories linger, softly laid.
Each heartbeat echoes, lost in time,
Silent tears, a mournful rhyme.

Ghostly tales of love still clung,
In every verse, a song unsung.
Yearning hearts beneath the sky,
Fade away, yet never die.

Winds of sorrow gently blow,
Through empty halls where passions flow.
A canvas stained with shades of gray,
Yet hope thrives in the midst of fray.

In the twilight, spirits soar,
In every sigh, they live once more.
These lines crafted from pain and grace,
Hold the memory, time can't erase.

Rhythm of Resilient Peaks

Mountains rise against the sky,
Against the storm, the strong must try.
Roots run deep through earth and stone,
In their shadows, we are not alone.

Echoes of the brave resound,
Voices rising from the ground.
In the struggle, we stand tall,
United, we shall never fall.

Beneath the weight of trials faced,
Strength is forged, our fears erased.
Each summit reached, a tale to share,
The rhythm beats, for those who dare.

Through valleys deep, we journey forth,
Finding light, embracing worth.
In every doubt, a fire ignites,
The peaks remind us of our fights.

The Silent Choir

Beneath the hush of stars above,
Whispers dance on wings of love.
Each note a dream, a thought set free,
In silent echoes, they find glee.

Harmonies drift through the night air,
Invisible bonds that we all share.
Songs of hope in shadows cast,
With every heartbeat, they hold fast.

Voices rise like morning light,
Filling spaces, gentle and bright.
In the silence, a song takes flight,
Binding souls in shared delight.

Together we weave a tale so grand,
In silent choir, we take a stand.
With breaths of calm, we softly sing,
In the quiet, our spirits cling.

Textures of Togetherness

In vibrant threads our stories weave,
Moments gleam, together we believe.
Joyful laughter, softest sighs,
In every glance, a bond that ties.

Hands entwined, we walk the street,
Building dreams with every beat.
Colors blend in perfect art,
Merging lives, never apart.

Where shadows fall, light blooms anew,
In unity, we find our view.
Through every storm, we stand as one,
Finding solace with the sun.

Textures rich, our lives embraced,
Shared moments wealth, intertwined and laced.
In the tapestry of night and day,
Together we shine, come what may.